TUNISIA CROCHET

Natalia Valentin

δelος

CAPE TOWN

© 1990 Delos Publishers, 40 Heerengracht, Cape Town

All rights reserved.
No part of this book may be reproduced or transmitted in any form or by any means, electronic or mechanical, including photocopying, recording or by any information storage and retrieval system, without the written permission of the publisher.

Also available in Afrikaans as **Tunisiese hekelwerk**

Photography by André Stander and Fido Kleovoulou
Illustrations by Philien Bakker
Cover design by Abie and Jasmine Fakier
Cover photographs: Suikerbossie restaurant
Models: Karin Wyma and Liezl Richter
Typography and production by Robert B. Wouterse
Set in 9 on 11 pt Helvetica DTP
Printed and bound by National Book Printers, Goodwood, Cape
First edition 1990

ISBN 1 86826 115 8

CONTENTS

Abbreviations *4*
Introduction *4*
History *4*
Basic steps *5*
General instructions *5*
Commonly used Tunisian stitches *7*
Finishing *13*

Patterns
Child's jacket *14*
Men's waistcoat *16*
Double-breasted jacket *18*
Girl's cardigan *19*
Ladies' long-line jacket *20*
Men's cardigan *22*
Men's button-neck pullover *24*
Soft mohair jacket *26*
Country-style cardigan *28*
Elegant edge-to-edge jacket *30*

INTRODUCTION

Tunisian crochet is a combination of knitting and crochet methods using a single, long hook. Many people who have been crocheting or knitting for years have never heard of this stitch.

I learnt this craft from my grandmother as a little girl, before I could crochet or knit, in my native country, Romania. It has always been taught by word of mouth and, except for some brief references in crochet books, I have never found any garment patterns specifically for this stitch.

The great interest and response shown by the public to my TV programmes and the publication of patterns in various local magazines encouraged me to write this book. I hope that in the end the readers will share my enthusiasm for this attractive and easy craft.

The great advantage of Tunisian crochet is that it produces a very strong and hard-wearing fabric which does not stretch, no matter how many times the garment is washed.

Tunisian fabrics have much more elasticity and pliability than crocheted ones and also offer a greater variety in stitch design. Beginners could start by mastering Tunisian crochet before the basic crochet stitches.

It is very easy to design your own patterns: the length of the chain determines the size of your garment. In this book, I have selected ten easy patterns using yarns readily available in local shops. Almost all of them can be made using only an 8 mm Tunisian hook.

Natalia Valentin

HISTORY

I would like to be able to tell you exactly how, when and why Tunisian crochet originated. However, the history of this craft is difficult to trace, mainly because the distinction between crochet and Tunisian stitch has not always been as clearly defined as it is today. The name crochet is derived from the French word "crochet" meaning "hook".

The evidence we have suggests that the Berbers (natives from North Africa, i.e. Tunisia, Algeria and Morocco) and sailors in medieval Europe, made rough garments and rugs from handspun wool using a bone hook fashioned by themselves.

There is also some evidence that a kind of Tunisian stitch may have been practised in pre-Columbian South America (Peru). This stitch was probably used before knitting and weaving. In the Middle Ages, when knitting was a guild craft and practised by men, the apprentice boys had to complete a blanket in Tunisian stitch besides various other garments.

This craft has been called, in turn, Russian work, German work and Tunisian work. The Americans call it Afghan stitch and it is very popular for knee-rugs.

During Victorian times many rugs and blankets were worked with a very long hook made of four parts screwed together. For a long period and for unknown reasons, Tunisian crochet was almost forgotten.

During the Second World War people once again started using Tunisian crochet for blankets, using a homemade wooden hook. Thereafter, during the '50s and '60s, knitting and crocheting came back into fashion, but the Tunisian stitch was still the Cinderella of the crochet craft.

ABBREVIATIONS

beg	begin	p	purl	tr	treble
C	contrast colour	patt	pattern/pattern stitch	T-kst	Tunisian knit stitch
ch	chain/chain stitch	rep	repeat	T-pst	Tunisian purl stitch
cont	continue	rnd(s)	round(s)	T-st	basic Tunisian stitch
dc	double crochet	rem	remain(ing)	T-tr	Tunisian treble
dec	decrease	RS	right side	vert	vertical
inc	increase	ss	slip stitch(es)	WS	wrong side
k	knit	st(s)	stitch(es)	yrh	yarn round hook
lp(s)	loop(s)	TH	Tunisian hook		
M	main colour	tog	together		

THE BASIC STEPS

HOLDING THE HOOK
Everyone has their own way of holding the hook and controlling the yarn. For Tunisian crochet the usual way of holding the hook is an overhand grip, almost as you would hold a knife.

MAKING A CHAIN
Tunisian crochet, like ordinary crochet, starts with a chain as the foundation. The chain should be formed loosely enough so that the hook can enter easily.

Step 1
A chain begins with a loop secured by a slip knot.

Step 2
Holding the slip knot between thumb and middle finger of left (or right) hand, push the hook forward, yarn round hook.

Step 3
Draw the yarn through the loop.

Step 4
Repeat 2nd and 3rd steps until you have the desired number of chains.

HINTS FOR LEFT-HANDERS
Place instruction books in front of a mirror and follow the illustrations in the "mirror image".

GENERAL INSTRUCTIONS

Tunisian crochet is done with a fairly long hook with a knob at one end to prevent the stitches from sliding off. Tunisian stitch usually starts with a base chain with the same number of chains as there are stitches required in the first row. The work is done on the right side without turning. What distinguishes one pattern stitch from another is the way in which the stitches are picked up on the forward row, and closed on the reverse row.

Whatever pattern stitch you use, nearly all patterns begin with the two basic rows of basic Tunisian stitch.

Because of the working method, Tunisian stitch sometimes produces a bias effect. This tendency can be overcome by working the stitches fairly loosely. Always pull the yarn round the hook adequately through the stitch and when working back from left to right; never pull the first stitch through tightly (you lower the height of the row).

SELECTING YARNS
The range of yarns is enormous and the choice of colour and quality is yours.

In texture and finish, yarns may be soft, hard, shiny, stiff, flexible, fluffy or lumpy, and are available in various degrees of thickness. The labels describing the thickness of the yarn as 3 and 4 ply, double-knit (DK), aran and chunky are only meant as a general guideline. The brand names are those of the yarns used for designing the garments in this book.

If you want to substitute, always use a yarn of the same thickness. Because yarns are sold by weight and not length, this can cause problems when trying to substitute another yarn for the specific quality given in a pattern. For example, pure wool is heavier than pure acrylic and therefore results in fewer meters in each ball of wool (you will require more yarn).

HOOKS
As mentioned before, Tunisian hooks were made from bone or wood in the past. Modern hooks are manufactured from lightweight materials. The metric figure is based on the exact diameter of the shank of the hook in millimeters: the larger the metric figure, the greater the diameter of the hook. Tunisian hooks are usually made in different lengths, such as 30 cm, 35 cm and 50 cm, to accommodate varying numbers of stitches.

TENSION
In a published pattern, the number of stitches and rows per 10 cm are given under the heading of "tension" and is a result of the combination of size of yarn, size of needle and the tightness or looseness with which you form your stitches. Ideally, a stitch should be loose enough to allow the hook to slip through easily.

There is no such thing as an "average tension". When beginning any pattern it is essential to work a tension sample, using the correct hook and yarn.

If your sample has more stitches, you are working too tightly. To correct this you should change to a larger hook. If your sample has fewer stitches, you are working too loosely and you should change to a smaller hook.

MAKING A TENSION SAMPLE
Using the specified yarn, hook size and pattern stitch, work a piece at least 15 cm square. Place the sample right side up on a smooth, flat surface. Place a ruler horizontally across the bottom of a row of stitches. Use pins to mark beginning and end of one 10 cm measurement. Count the number of stitches between the pins. This will give the figure for the number of stitches of the sample. Place the ruler vertically along one side of a column of stitches. Mark out 10 cm with pins and count the number of rows.

MEASUREMENTS

After choosing the garment you want to make, you must first decide which size to follow. Sizes are given according to bust (chest) measurements. Choose which size to make by comparing the measurements to a similar garment you have that fits comfortably.

When reading a pattern, make sure you pay attention to *actual measurements* or *garment measurements*. It means that if you follow the instructions given for that particular size, the end-product will be that shown in "actual measurement".

Please note: Patterns in four sizes: first, second, third and fourth figures refer to 1st (2nd, 3rd and 4th sizes). One figure only refers to all sizes. The same rule applies to two or three sizes.

INCREASING

A single stitch can be increased at each end of the collecting row.

At the right-hand edge, make one chain then insert the hook behind the vertical thread of the first stitch (edge stitch), yarn round hook and draw a loop through, continue in pattern to end of row.

At the extreme left-hand edge, work into each of two vertical strands of yarn.

To increase two or more stitches at the right-hand edge, make the required number of chains, then work basic stitch into each chain, then into edge stitch and continue in pattern to end.

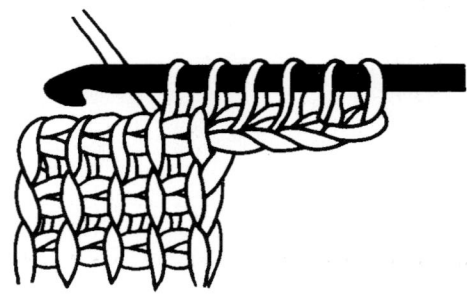

To increase two or more stitches at the left-hand edge, use a separate length of yarn and make the required number of chains and leave for the time being. Work in pattern to the end of the row, then work in basic stitch into each chain of separate chain.

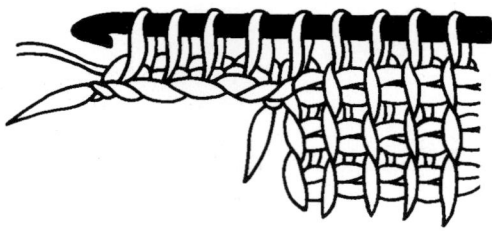

A single stitch can be increased at any given point in the forward row by working the increased stitch under the horizontal loop which lies between two vertical loops and drawing an extra loop through on the hook.

DECREASING

A single stitch can be decreased at each end of the forward row.

At the right-hand edge, insert the hook through second and third stitch and work the two stitches together.

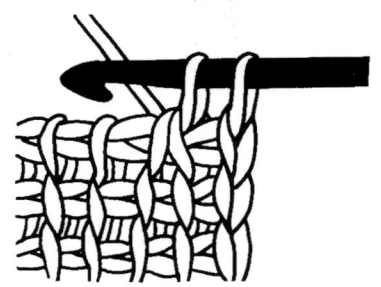

At the left-hand edge, work two stitches together before the last stitch. A single stitch can also be decreased at any given point in the forward row by working two vertical threads together.

To decrease two or more stitches at the right-hand edge, slip stitch along the number of stitches to be decreased, then continue in pattern to end.

At the end of the row, leave the number of stitches to be decreased unworked. Before making up the garment, join a separate length of yarn and work one slip stitch into each decreased stitch to avoid holes.

FASTEN OFF

Work one row of slip stitches into vertical loops of last row.

WORKING A BUTTONHOLE IN TUNISIAN STITCH

Work a forward row to the position where the buttonhole is required, wind yarn round hook for the required number of stitches for the buttonhole, miss this number of stitches in the previous row and continue in pattern to end. In the following row, work off each loop of yarn as if it were a stitch.

WORKING A BUTTONHOLE IN DOUBLE CROCHET STITCH

Work until the position for buttonhole is reached, work the number of chains in the desired position and miss the same number of double crochet stitches in the previous row. In the next row, work one double crochet stitch into each chain.

GENERAL INSTRUCTIONS FOR CROCHET STITCHES USED IN THIS BOOK

Slip stitch (ss): Insert hook into a stitch, yarn round hook and draw a loop through stitch and through loop on hook. Repeat to end. Use slip stitch for fastening off and decreasing more than one stitch.

Double crochet (dc): Insert hook into a stitch, yarn round hook, draw a loop, yarn round hook and draw through two loops.

COMMONLY USED TUNISIAN STITCHES

PLAIN OR BASIC TUNISIAN STITCH (T-st)

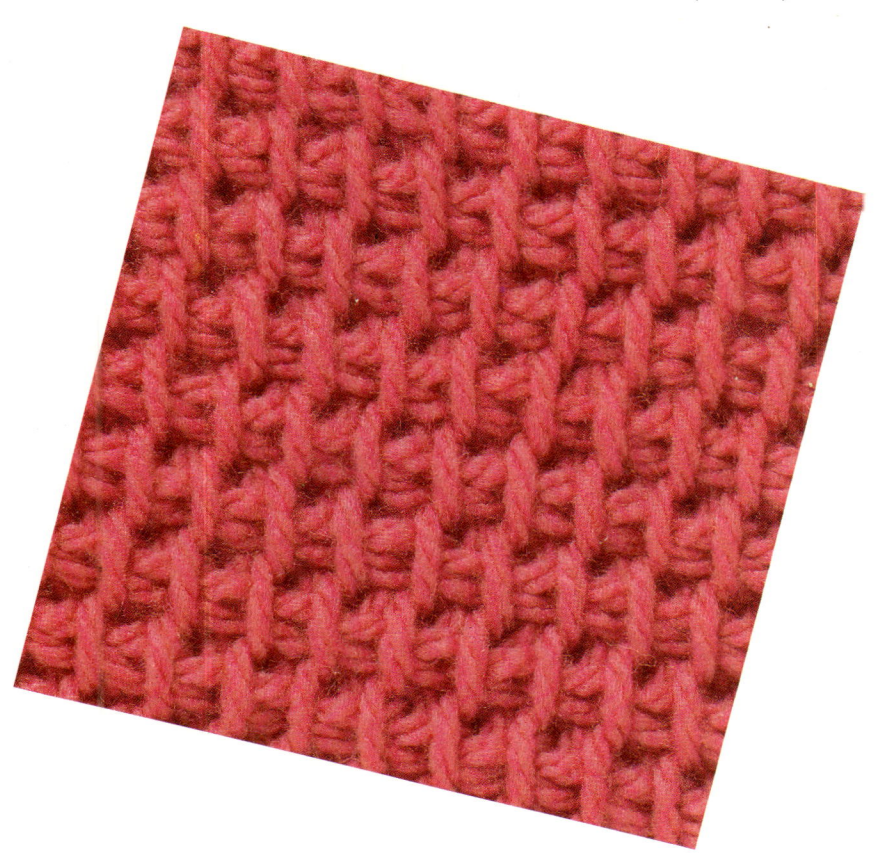

Make any number of ch (chain stitches).
1st row: Insert hook into 2nd ch from hook, yrh (yarn round hook) and draw a lp (loop) through ch, *insert hook into next ch, yrh and draw a lp through ch. Rep (repeat) from * to end. Do not turn work. The number of lps on the hook should be the same as the starting ch.

2nd row: Working from left to right, yrh and draw through 1st lp, *yrh and draw through 2 lps on hook. Rep from * until 1 lp is left on hook. The lp left on hook is the 1st st (stitch) of next row. This is the **reverse** row.

3rd row: Insert hook into 2nd vert (vertical) lp from right to left, yrh and draw a lp through. Rep from * into each vert thread to end. Do not turn. This is the **forward** row.

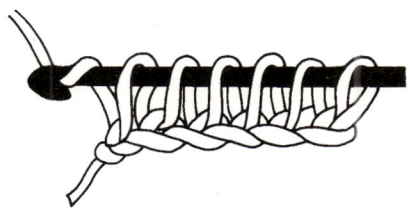

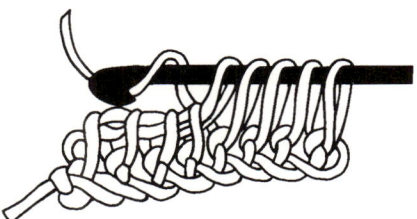

Note: It is very important to pull through 1 lp only at the beg (beginning) of the reverse row, otherwise the fabric will warp.

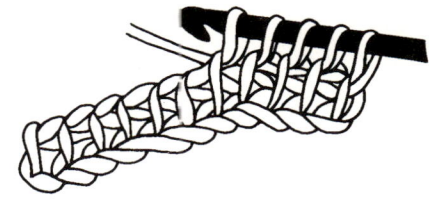

Note: At the end of this row, be sure to insert the hook through the centre of the last lp at the edge so that there are 2 vert strands of yarn at the extreme left-hand edge. Check that the number of sts is correct, as it is easy to miss the last st of this patt (pattern).
4th row: As 2nd row.
3rd and 4th rows form patt.

TUNISIAN KNIT STITCH *(T-kst)*

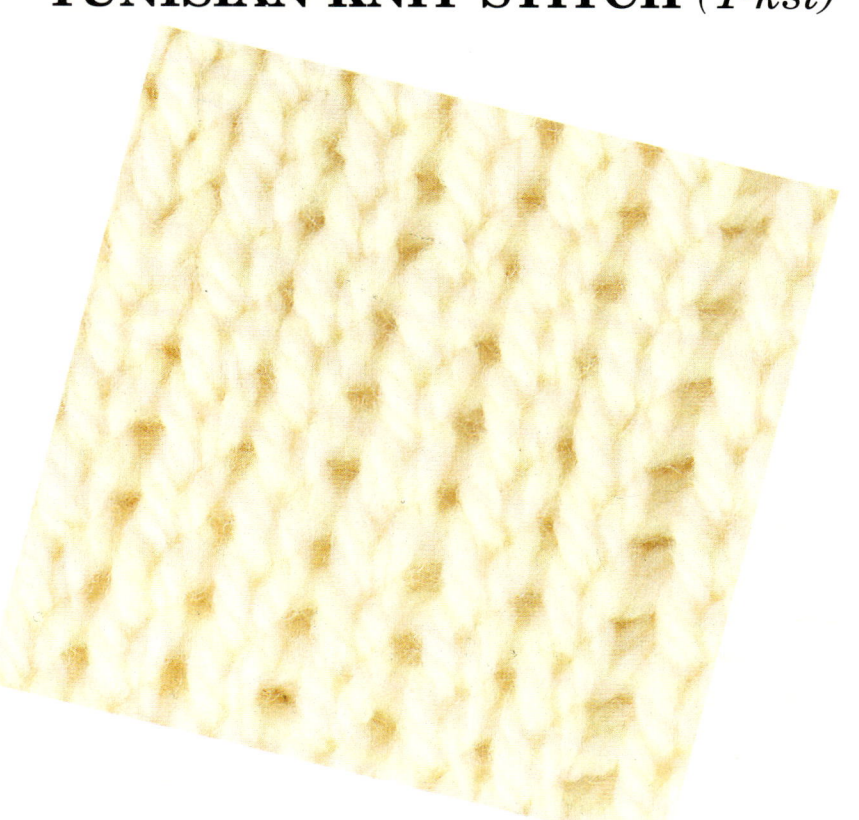

Work 2 rows in T-st.
3rd row: *Insert hook from right to left in centre of next vert lp, yrh and draw a lp through (the centre of the lp can be seen if you separate the 2 yarns using thumb and 3rd finger of left hand, or right hand for left-handers). Rep from * to end of row.
4th row: As 2nd row of T-st.
3rd and 4th rows form patt.
This patt looks like knitted stitch, except that it is thicker.

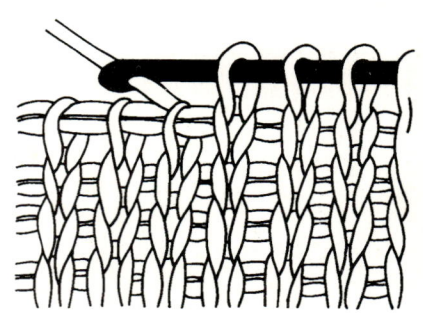

TUNISIAN PURL STITCH *(T-pst)*

Work 2 rows in T-st.
3rd row: *Holding yarn in front of work as for purl st in knitting, insert hook from right to left under next vert thread, yrh and draw through a lp. Rep from * to end.
4th row: As 2nd row of T-st.
3rd and 4th rows form patt.

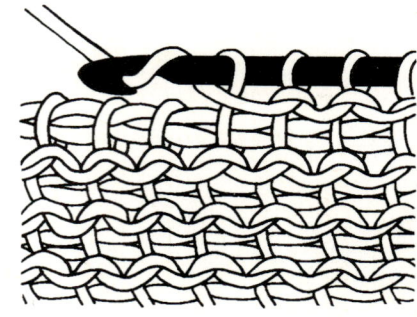

DOUBLE TUNISIAN STITCH

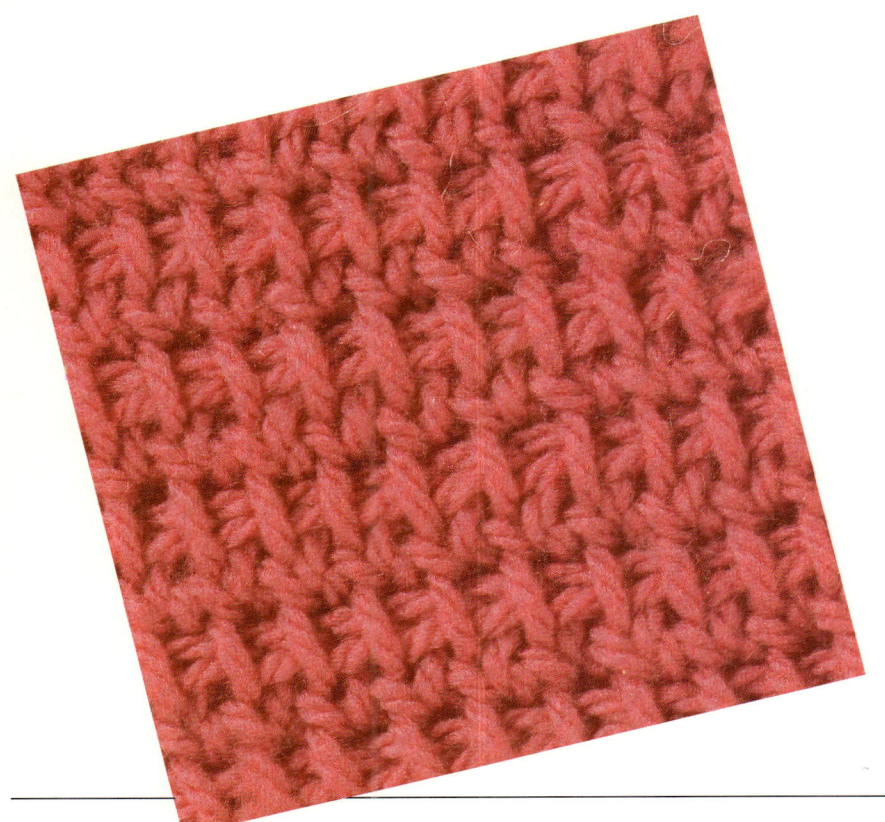

Work 2 rows in T-st.
3rd row: Ch 1, *into next vert thread work 1 T-st, then ch 1. Rep from * to last st. Work last st as T-st.
4th row: As 2nd row of T-st.
3rd and 4th rows form patt.

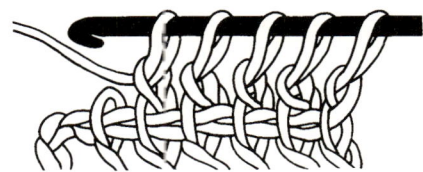

CROSSED TUNISIAN STITCH

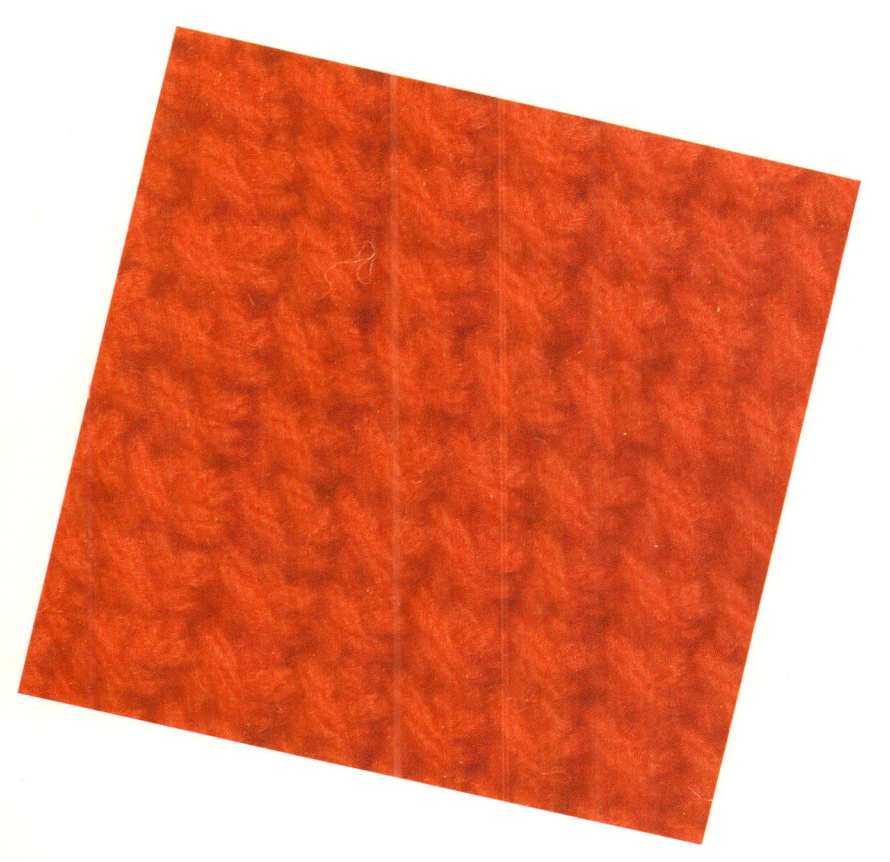

Work 2 rows in T-st.
3rd row: *Insert hook from right to left under 2nd vert thread, yrh and draw through a lp, return to 1st vert thread, insert hook, yrh, draw through a lp. Rep from * to end.
4th row: Yrh, draw through 1st lp, *yrh, draw through 3 lps. Rep from * to end.
3rd and 4th rows form patt.

TWO-COLOUR TUNISIAN STITCH

Work in T-st throughout, changing colours as follows:
Ch in A
1st row: A
2nd row: B
3rd row: B
4th row: A
These 4 rows form patt.

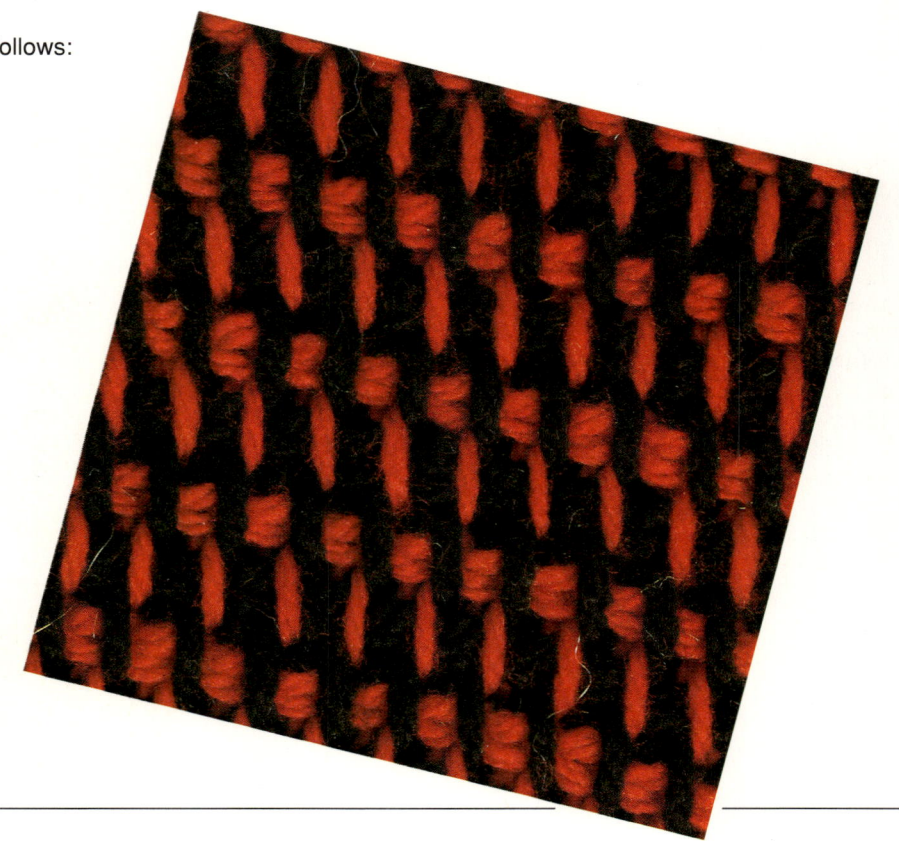

TUNISIAN TREBLE *(T-tr)*

Work 2 rows in T-st.
3rd row: 1 ch to count as 1st st, *yrh, insert hook from right to left under vert thread of next st, yrh and draw a lp through, yrh and draw through 2 lps on hook. Rep from * to end.

4th row: As 2nd row of T-st.
3rd and 4th rows form patt.

TUNISIAN FAN STITCH *(worked over 14 sts + 2)*

With A, work 2 rows in T-st.
3rd to 10th row: Rep 3rd and 4th rows of T-st.
11th row: With B, 1 edge st, *work 1 T-st into each of next 7 sts, miss 3 sts, yrh, insert hook from front to back (as for knit stitch) into next st and work 7 tr (trebles) into 1 st, keeping lp from each tr on hook (called fan), miss 3 sts*, 1 edge st. Rep from * to *.
12th row: As 2nd row of T-st.
13th to 20th row: With A, rep 3rd and 4th rows of T-st.
21st row: Using B, 1 edge st, *miss 3 sts, 1 fan into next st, miss 3 sts, 1 T-st into each of next 7 sts*, 1 edge st. Rep from * to *.
22nd row: As 2nd row of T-st.
Rep these 22 rows for patt.

TWO-COLOUR WAVE PATTERN *(worked over 10 sts + 2)*

With A, work 2 rows in T-st.
3rd row: With B, insert hook from right to left under vert thread of next st and slip it on hook (= 1 ss), *1 T-st into each of next 2 sts, 1 tr into each of next 4 sts, 1 T-st into each of next 2 sts, slip next 2 sts onto hook*, 1 edge st. Rep from * to *.
4th row: With B, as 2nd row of T-st.
5th to 8th row: Using A, as 3rd and 4th row of T-st.
9th row: Using B, 1 ch counting as 1 tr, 1 tr into next st, *2 T-sts, 2 ss, 4 tr*. Rep from * to *.
10th row: As 2nd row.
Rep these 10 rows for patt.

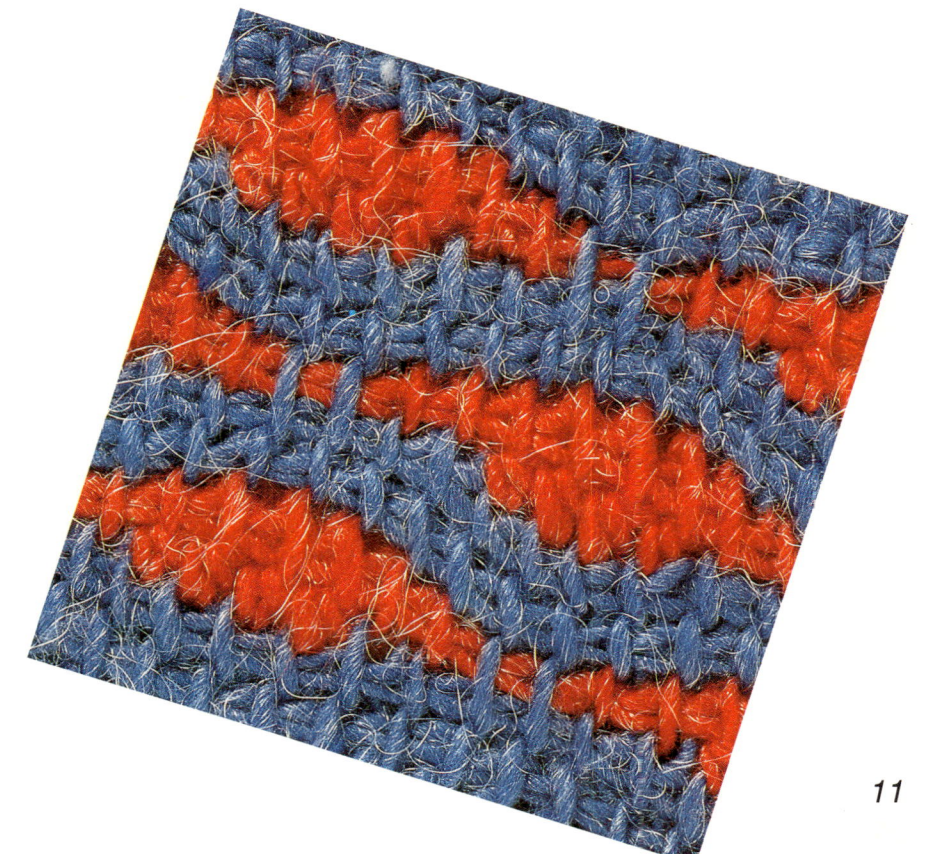

TUNISIAN BRICK PATTERN

Work 2 rows in T-st, using A.
3rd to 6th row: Using B, as 3rd and 4th rows of T-st.
7th row: Using A, 1 T-st into next st, *yrh, insert hook from right to left under vert thread of next st but 4 rows below (i.e. the 1st row in A) and draw a lp, yrh and draw through 2 lps on hook (= 1 long tr), 1 T-st into each of next 3 sts*. Rep from * to *.
8th row: Using A, as 2nd row of T-st.
9th to 12th row: Using B, as 3rd and 4th rows of T-st.
13th row: Using A, 1 long tr into 2nd st from hook, *1 T-st into each of next 3 sts, 1 long tr into next st*. Rep from * to *.
14th row: Using A, as 2nd row of T-st.
Rep these 14 rows for patt.

TUNISIAN ARAN PATTERN *(worked over 7 sts + 2)*

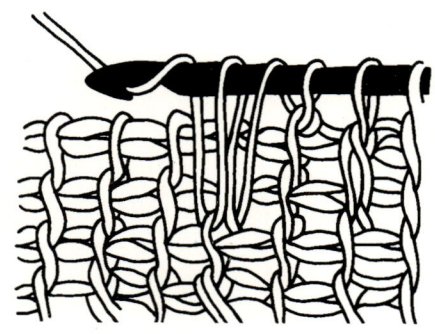

Work 2 rows in T-st.
3rd to 8th row: As 3rd and 4th rows of T-st.
9th row: 1 edge st, *[yrh] twice, miss 3 sts, insert hook from right to left under vert thread of next st but 6 rows below (i.e. 3rd row of patt) and draw a long lp, yrh, draw yarn through 2 lps, yrh, draw yarn through 2 lps (= long tr – see diagram), miss st behind tr, work 1 T-st into each of next 5 sts and work a 2nd long tr into same st as 1st tr, miss st behind tr, 1 edge st.

10th row: As 2nd row of T-st.
11th to 14th row: T-st.
15th row: Edge st, 1 T-st into each of next 3 sts, yrh, insert hook from right to left under vert thread of next st 6 rows below (i.e. 9th row of patt) and draw a lp, yrh and draw through 2 lps (1 tr). Work 2 more tr into same st, keeping last lp of each tr on hook. Yrh and draw through last 3 lps (= 1 bobble), miss st behind bobble, work to end.

16th row: As 2nd row of T-st.
17th to 20th row: T-st.
21st row: Edge st, 1 bobble into next st (6 rows below), miss st behind bobble, 1 T-st into each of next 5 sts, 1 bobble into next st, miss st behind bobble, work to end.
22nd row: As 2nd row of T-st.
23rd to 26th row: T-st.
27th row: As 15th row.
28th row: As 2nd row of T-st.

FINISHING

Blocking and seaming will add a professional touch to your Tunisian garment. It takes far more time than one would imagine, but as the whole appearance of the garment depends on how well it is sewn up and edged, it is time well spent. Before blocking, darn stray ends of yarn neatly into the WS (wrong side) of the fabric with a blunt needle.

BLOCKING

Pressing is not recommended. To put pieces into shape before they can be joined together, place a folded blanket covered with a damp towel or cloth on the floor or on a table. Pin the pieces of the garment with RS (right side) down to the cloth, using rustproof pins. Make sure that each piece of the garment is the correct shape and size, and that all rows and lines of sts are straight. Cover with a damp cloth or towel and leave them for a few hours. Remove the cloth and allow work to dry. Unpin.

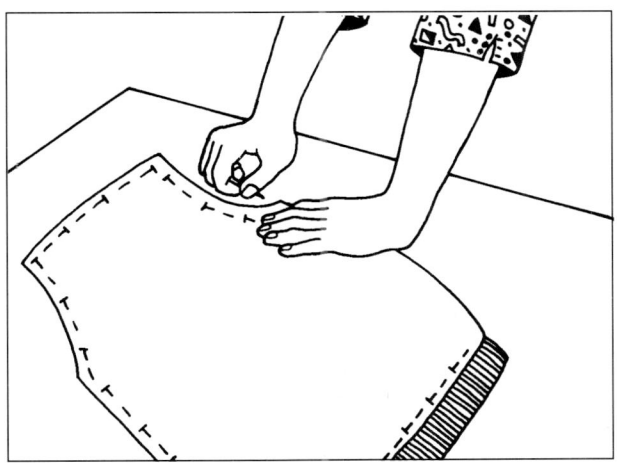

SEWING UP

The Tunisian crochet edges are often uneven, especially when several different stitches have been combined. Keeping work flat, work a row of dc (double crochet) along the edges. Experiment to see which sewing method is best for the seams.

Backstitch: Makes a strong but bulky seam.

Edge-to-edge seam: Produces a flat, invisible join.

Grafting or weaving: Used in Tunisian garments, this gives a neat and professional appearance to side edges. Place the pieces with RS facing and edges touching. Thread a blunt needle with matching yarn and weave tog (together) from side to side, matching rows.

Slipstitch seam: This is the quickest method for Tunisian and crocheted garments. Use a 3 mm crochet hook for a DK yarn and a 4 mm crochet hook for a chunky yarn. Place pieces with RS together. Insert hook from front to back through the edge sts of both pieces, yrh and draw through to make a ss. Rep to end, taking care not to work too tightly.

EDGINGS

The success of a garment also depends on its neat, even edgings. Both sides of the edging must match exactly. Pick up about 1 st from each T-st and 1 st from every 2nd row. You may crochet or knit the edges separately and sew them on. A knitted rib will give a tight, smart finish to a Tunisian garment. The most basic crocheted edging consists of a single row or rnd (round) of dc. Instructions usually call for a dc to be worked "evenly along edge", that means to work loosely so that the edge is not pulled together. To pick up sts, insert hook from front to back into edge st and work a dc. There are no easy rules to guide you in making borders. You must be prepared to unravel and try again. To form a "corner", you must inc (increase) or dec (decrease) according to the instructions of the patt.

Corded edge or crab stitch: This is a very decorative twisted edging made by working in dc from left to right as follows:

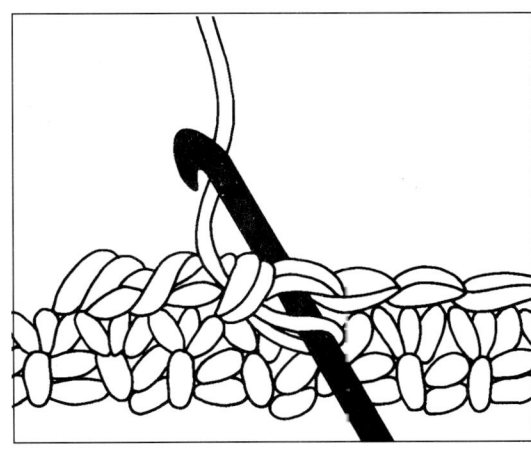

Work 1 row of dc as a basic row, do not turn. Working from left to right, *insert hook into next st to the right, yrh, pull lp through, yrh, pull through 2 lps on hook*. Rep from * to * to end.

Knitted edging: This offers an effective alternative to crochet edging and will provide a softer and flexible finishing edge. Pick up the number of sts required in patt along the foundation row or along a side row. The sts must be spread evenly along the edge. Insert the point of the knitting needles through the edge of fabric, wind yarn around needle, draw the yarn through (= 1 st). Cont in the same way until the required number of sts are on the needle.

CHILD'S JACKET

Measurements
To fit: 56(61;66;71) cm chest
Garment measures: 61(66;71;76) cm
Length from shoulder: 38(42;46;49) cm
Sleeve seam: 23(27;31;35) cm

Materials
Pingouin Frosty (50 g): 3(3;4;4) balls in M (main colour)
1 ball in C (contrast colour)
One 8 mm TH
One 4 mm crochet hook
4(4;5;5) buttons

Tension: 13 sts = 10 cm with TH over T-st

Back
With M and TH, ch 38(42;46;50) and work in T-st until back measures 38(42;46;49) cm from starting ch, ending with a reverse row. Fasten off.

Right front
**With C, ch 19(21;23;25) and work 1st and 2nd row of T-st. Join M (draw new colour through last lp on hook and carry yarn not in use loosely at side of work).
3rd to 6th row: T-st**.
7th row: (C) 1 T-st into 2nd and 3rd sts from hook, *yrh, insert hook under vert thread of next st but 4 rows below (i.e. 1st row in C) and draw a lp, yrh and draw through 2 lps on hook (called 1 long tr). Work 1 T-st into each of next 3 sts*.
Sizes 61 and 71: Rep from * to * to end of row.
Sizes 66 and 76: Rep from * to * to last 2 sts, 1 long tr into next st, 1 T-st into last st.
8th row: (C) Work a reverse row.
9th to 12th row: (M) T-st.
13th row: (C) 1 long tr into 2nd st from hook, *1 T-st into each of next 3 sts, 1 long tr into next st 4 rows below*. Rep from * to * to last 1(3;1;3) sts, T-st to end.
14th row: (C) Reverse row. These 14 rows form brick patt.
Cont in patt until work measures about 5(6;6;7) cm less than back to shoulder, ending with 8th or 14th row of patt.

Shape neck
Keeping continuity of patt, dec 3(3;3;4) sts at beg of next row, patt to end. Work a reverse row.
Next row: Dec 2 sts, patt to end. Work a reverse row. Cont to dec 1 st at neck edge as before until 11(13;14;15) sts rem on hook, then cont in patt until front matches back to shoulder. Fasten off.

Left front
Work as right front from ** to **
7th row: Work as 13th row of brick patt, then cont in patt from 3rd to 14th row until left front matches right front to neck shaping. Shape at end of forward row, leaving sts to be dec unworked. Work to match right front. Fasten off.

Sleeves
With M, ch 21(25;25;27). Work 4 rows in T-st. Join C and work 2 rows (a forward and a reverse row). Work from 3rd to 8th row in brick patt, then cont only in M and T-st.
Next row: Inc 1 st at each end.
Next row: Reverse row.
Next 4 rows: T-st.
Rep last 6 rows until 38(40;42;44) sts, then cont until work measures 23(27;31;35) cm from starting ch, ending with a reverse row. Fasten off.

To make up
Block pieces and pull into shape. Join shoulder seams. Set in sleeves. Join side and sleeve seams.

Borders
With 4 mm crochet hook, C and RS facing, start at right side seam, work 1 rnd of dc along lower edge of right front, up right front edge, along back of neck edge, down left front edge and along lower edge of left front and back. Work 3 dc into 1 st at corners. Close rnd with a ss, do not turn. Mark position of buttons: the first about 1,5 cm below neck edge and the last about 4 cm above lower edge. Work 1 rnd making 4(4;5;5) buttonholes on right or left front border. To make a buttonhole: miss 2 sts (see General Instructions). Work 2 more rnds in dc. Do not turn. Work 1 rnd of crab st.

Sleeve edge
With C, 4 mm crochet hook and RS facing, start at seam edge, work 3 rnds of dc, ending with 1 rnd of crab st. Fasten off. Sew on buttons.

MEN'S WAISTCOAT

Measurements
To fit: 97(102;107;112) cm chest
Length from shoulder: 62(63;64;65) cm

Materials
Elle Tweed (50 g): 6(7;7;8) balls
One 8 cm TH
One 3,5 mm circular knitting needle
4(4;5;5) buttons

Tension: 13 sts = 10 cm with TH over T-st

Back
With TH, ch 66(70;74;78) and work in T-st until work measures 33 cm from starting ch, ending with a reverse row.

Shape armholes
Next row: Dec 3(3;4;4) sts at beg and end of row.
Next row: Work a reverse row.
Dec 1 st at each edge in every forward row until 52(56;58;62) sts rem. Cont in T-st until work measures 56(57;58;58) cm from starting ch, ending with a reverse row. Fasten off.

Right front
Ch 33(35;37;39) and work in T-st until work measures 21(22;23;23) cm from starting ch. Place a marker at right-hand edge of work.

Shape front edge
Next row (forward row): Miss first st, work next 2 sts tog (1 dec), T-st to end.
Work a reverse row.
Next 10 rows: T-st.
Rep last 12 rows 13(14;14;15) times. At same time, when work measures 33 cm from starting ch ending with a reverse row, **shape armhole:**
Dec 3(3;4;4) sts at left-hand edge of work by leaving sts unworked, then dec 1 st at same edge in next 4 forward rows. Working straight at armhole edge, cont to dec at front until 13(14;15;16) sts left. Work to match back to shoulder, ending with a reverse row. Fasten off.

Left front
Work as given for right front, reversing shapings. Using a separate length of yarn, work ss over sts left unworked from armhole shaping.

To make up and borders
Block pieces and pull into shape. Join shoulder and side seams.

Armhole borders (2)
With RS facing and 3,5 mm circular needle, start at side seam and pick up and k110(110;114;114) sts evenly around armhole edge and work in rounds 2,5 cm in k1, p1 rib. Cast off in rib.

Welt
With RS facing and 3,5 mm circular needle, start at lower edge of left front and pick up and k55(58;60;64) sts from left front, 110(116;120;128) sts from back and 55(58;60;64) sts from right front. Work in rows for 6(6;6;7) cm in single rib, as given for armhole border. Cast off in rib.

Front and neck border
With RS facing and circular needle, start at lower edge of right front and pick up and k130(132;134;136) sts up right front edge (about 21 sts for every 10 cm), 42(42;43;44) sts along back of neck and 130(132;134;136) sts down left front edge to cast off edge of welt. Work 4 rows in single rib. Mark position of buttons: the first 1 cm from lower edge and the last at beg of front shaping (see marker). Divide other 2(2;3;3) buttonholes evenly between.

Buttonholes
In first row cast off 2 sts, in second row cast on 2 sts over cast off sts. Work 4 more rows in rib. Cast off in rib. Sew on buttons.

DOUBLE-BREASTED JACKET

(Photo on front cover)

Measurements
To fit: 81(86;91;97) cm bust
Garment measures: 86(91;97;102) cm
Length from shoulder: 56(56;57;57) cm
Sleeve seam: 47(47;48;48) cm

Materials
Robin Fascination Fashion DK (100 g):
3(3;4;4) balls
One 8 mm TH
One 3,75 mm circular knitting needle
One 4 mm crochet hook
4 buttons

Tension: 14 sts = 10 cm with TH over T-st

Back
With TH, ch 60(64;68;72) and work in T-st until back measures 56(56;57;57) cm from starting ch, ending with a reverse row. Fasten off.

Right front
Ch 20(22;24;25) and work in T-st as given for back until work measures 56(56;57;57) cm, ending with a reverse row. Fasten off.

Left front
Work as right front.

Sleeves
Starting from sleeve top, ch 58(58;62;64) and work 4 rows in T-st. Dec 1 st at each end of next row. Work a reverse row. Work 4 rows in T-st. Rep last 6 rows until 32(34;34;36) sts on hook. Work straight until sleeve measures 47(47;48;48) cm from starting ch, ending with a reverse row. Fasten off.
Block pieces to measurements before working the collar.

Front border and collar
Join shoulder seams. With RS facing and 3,75 mm circular needle, pick up and k120(120;124;124) sts up right front edge from starting ch of front to shoulder; pick up and k30(30;34;34) sts across back of neck and 120(120;124;124) sts down left front edge to starting ch of left front. Work in rows in k2, p2 rib as follows:
1st row: On WS [p2, k2] to last 2 sts, p2.
2nd row: [K2, p2] to last 2 sts, k2.
Rep last 2 rows until rib measures 2,5 cm, ending with a WS row.
1st buttonhole row: Rib 6 sts, cast off 2 sts, rib 20 sts (counting st from casting off), cast off 2 sts, rib to end.
2nd buttonhole row: Rib to end, casting on 2 sts over cast off st of previous row. Cont in rib for 9(10;11;12) cm, ending with a WS row. Rep 1st and 2nd buttonhole rows, then work 2,5 cm in rib. Cast off in rib.

To make up
Set in sleeves. Join side and sleeve seams. Sew on buttons.

Edgings
Lower edge: With RS facing and 4,5 mm crochet hook, start at 1st row of rib, work 1 row of dc along lower edge of fronts and back by working 1 dc into each vert thread. Do not turn, ch 1 and work 1 row of crab st into each dc. Fasten off.

Sleeves: With RS facing and crochet hook, start at sleeve seam and work 1 rnd in dc along lower edge of sleeve. Close rnd with a ss, do not turn. Ch 1 and work 1 rnd in crab st. Close with a ss. Fasten off.

GIRL'S CARDIGAN

(Photo on back cover)

Measurements
To fit: 56(61;66;71;76) cm chest
Garment measures: 61(66;71;76;81) cm
Length from shoulder: 38(42;46;49;53) cm
Sleeve seam: 23(27;31;35;39) cm

Materials
Pingouin Tivoli (50 g): 3(4;4;5;5) balls
One 3 mm TH
One 3,5 mm crochet hook
5(5;5;6;6) buttons

Tension: 14 sts = 10 cm with TH over T-st

Main part (worked in 1 piece to armholes)
With TH, ch 82(90;94;102;110) and work 1st and 2nd rows of T-st. Work in rib patts as follows:
1st row: Miss 1st st (edge st), 1 T-kst (Tunisian knit stitch) into next st, *1 T-pst (Tunisian purl stitch) into each of next 2 sts, 1 T-kst into each of next 2 sts*. Rep from * to * to end of row. Work a reverse row.
Rep last 2 rows for 5(5;5;6;6) cm, ending with a reverse row. Cont in T-st until work measures 24(27;31;33;36) cm from starting ch, ending with a reverse row.

Divide for armholes
Next row: Work 17(19;20;22;23) sts in T-st for right front, leaving rem sts unworked. Work a reverse row and cont in T-st until work measures 9(10;10;10;11) cm from armhole division, ending with a reverse row.

Shape neck
Next row: Dec 3 sts, T-st to end. Work a reverse row.
Next row: Dec 2 sts, T-st to end. Work a reverse row.
Dec 1 st at same edge until 10(11;13;14;14) sts rem. Work straight until armhole measures 14(15;15;16;17) cm. Fasten off. With RS facing, return to rem sts, rejoin yarn at right armhole and cast off 7(7;8;8;9) sts (work 1 ss into each of next 7(7;8;8;9) sts), work 34(38;38;42;46) sts in T-st, leaving rem sts. Cont over these sts for back until work measures as right front to shoulder. Fasten off. With RS facing, join yarn to rem sts, cast off 7(7;8;8;9) sts and work left side of front to match right side.

Sleeves
Starting from sleeve top, ch 40(42;42;46;48) and work in T-st for 2,5(2,5;3;3;3,5) cm. Mark last row at both ends.
Next row: Dec 1 st at each end.
Next row: Work a reverse row.
Next 4 rows: T-st.
Rep last 6 rows until 30(30;32;34;38) sts rem on hook, work without shaping until sleeve seam measures 19(23;27;30;34) cm from starting ch, ending with a reverse row.
Next row: Work a forward row, dec evenly 10(10;12;12;14) sts along row (see General Instructions for decreasing). Work a reverse row.
Next row: Work in rib patt as given for welt (at beginning of main part) until sleeve seam measures 23(27;31;35;39) cm from starting ch. Fasten off.

Collar
Ch 46(46;50;50;50) and work in rib patt as given for welt for 2 cm.
Next row: Patt in rib, inc 1 st into each purl section. Patt will read 2 T-kst, 3 T-pst. Cont in rib as set until collar measures 7(7;7;7;8) cm from starting ch. Fasten off.

Front borders
With RS facing and 3,5 mm crochet hook, starting at neck edge, work 5 rows in dc, along left front edge.
Buttonhole border: Mark position of buttons: the first 1 cm below neck edge and the last 1,5 cm above starting ch. Work 2 rows in dc. Into 3rd row make 5(5;5;6;6) buttonholes (see General Instructions). For each buttonhole miss 2 sts. Work 2 more rows in dc. Fasten off.

To make up
Block pieces and pull into shape. Join sleeve seams to markers. Set in sleeves. Sew collar in position, with starting ch at neck edge. Sew on buttons.

LADIES' LONG-LINE JACKET

Measurements
To fit: 81-91(97-102) cm bust
Garment measures: 100(110) cm
Length from shoulder: 77 cm
Sleeve length: 46 cm

Materials
Elle Harlequin (50 g): 15(17) balls
One 8 mm TH
One 6 mm crochet hook

Tension: 11 sts = 10 cm with TH over T-st

Yoke and sleeves are worked in 1 piece, starting at left wrist. With TH, ch 50 and work 46 cm in T-st. Place a marker at end of last row (end of left sleeve). Work 17(19) cm from marker, ending with a reverse row.

Divide for neck
Next row: Work 22 sts in T-st, cast off next 3 sts (work 1 ss into each of next 3 sts), complete row. Cont over rem 25 sts for left side of front yoke. Work 8(9) cm from neck division, ending with a reverse row. Fasten off.

Right side of front yoke
Ch 25 and work in T-st for 8(9) cm, ending with a reverse row. Ch 3 at end of last row and leave this side unworked. With RS facing, rejoin yarn at neck division and work over 22 sts for 16(18) cm to complete back of yoke, ending with a reverse row.

Joining row
With RS facing, work 22 sts from back yoke in T-st, draw a lp from each of the 3 ch from right front yoke and cont over 25 sts from right front yoke to end of row. Cont over 50 sts until work measures 17(19) cm from joining row. Place a marker at both ends of last row. Work 46 cm from markers, ending with a reverse row. Fasten off.

Back
Ch 54(60) and work 10(11) cm in T-st, ending with a reverse row.
Next row: *Miss 1st st, work next 2 sts together (1 dec), work to last 3 sts, work next 2 sts tog (1 dec), work to end. Work a reverse row. Work 10 cm in T-st*. Rep from * to * twice more = 48(54) sts. Cont straight until back measures 54 cm from starting ch. Fasten off.

Left front
Ch 27(30) and work 10 cm in T-st.
Next row: *Miss 1st st, work next 2 sts tog (1 dec), work to end. Work a reverse row. Work another 10 cm in T-st*. Rep from * to * until 24(27) sts rem. Cont straight until front measures 54 cm. Fasten off.

Right front
Work as given for left front, dec at left-hand edge of work.

To make up
Block pieces to measurements. Join back to back of yoke between markers. Join left and right fronts to yoke between markers. Join side and sleeve seams.

Edging
With RS facing and 6 mm crochet hook, start at right seam and work 3 rnds of dc. Keep edges flat and work 3 dc into each st at corners. Without turning, work 1 row in crab st. Close with a ss and fasten off.

Sleeves edging: Work 3 rnds in dc and 1 rnd of crab st around lower edge of sleeves.

Yoke edging: With RS facing and 6 mm crochet hook, work 1 row crab st along joining seam of front and back yoke.

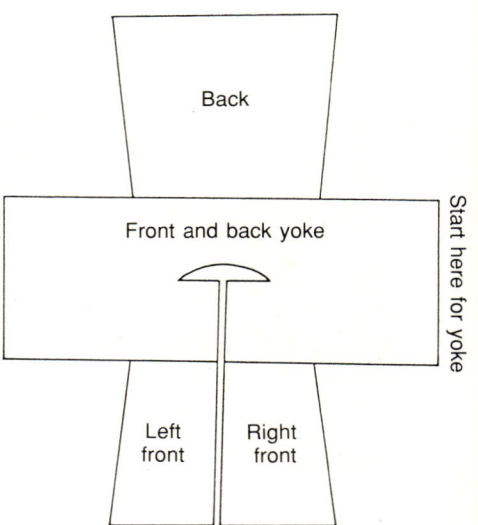

MEN'S CARDIGAN

Measurements
To fit: 97(102;107;112) cm chest
Length from shoulder: 62(63;64;65) cm
Sleeve seam: 49(49;51;51) cm

Materials
Jaeger Morland Chunky 90% wool (50 g): 15(16;17;17) balls
One 8 mm TH
One 5 mm crochet hook
5 buttons

Tension: 12 sts = 10 cm with TH over patt

Back
With TH, ch 62(66;68;72) and work 1st and 2nd rows of T-st.
3rd row: Work 1 T-kst, 1 T-st (see instructions for Tunisian stitches).
4th row: Reverse row. This is the main patt.
Rep 3rd and 4th rows for patt until work measures 62(63;64;65) cm from starting ch, ending with a reverse row. Fasten off.

Left front
Ch 31(33,35,37) and work 1st and 2nd rows of T-st.
3rd row: Miss 1st st, [1 T-st, 1 T-kst] over 15(17;17;19) sts including edge st, 7 T-sts over next 7 sts (front panel), 1 T-kst, T-st to last st, 1 T-st.
4th row: Reverse row.
5th to 8th row: As 3rd and 4th rows.
9th row: Work in main patt as set over 15(17;17;19) sts, 3 T-st into next 3 sts, yrh, insert hook from right to left under vert thread of next st 6 rows below and draw a lp, yrh and draw through 2 lps (1 tr). Work 2 more tr in same way in same st, keeping last lp of each tr on hook. Yrh and draw through 3 lps (1 bobble), miss st behind bobble, 3 T-st over next 3 sts, cont in main patt to end.
10th row: Reverse row.
11th to 14th row: As 3rd and 4th rows of left front patt.
15th row: 15(17;17;19) in main patt, 1 bobble 6 rows below, 5 T-st, 1 bobble 6 rows below, main patt to end.
16th row: Reverse row.
17th to 20th row: As 3rd and 4th rows of left front patt.
21st row: As 9th row.
22nd row: Reverse row.
23rd to 32nd row: As 3rd and 4th rows of left front patt.
33rd row: 15(17;17;19) in main patt, miss 3 sts, [yrh] twice, insert hook from right to left under vert thread of next st but 6 rows below and draw a long lp, yrh, draw yarn through 2 lps, yrh, draw through 2 lps (called a long tr), 5 T-st, 1 long tr into same st as first tr, main patt to end.
34th row: Reverse row. Rep patt from 3rd to 34th row for front panel until work measures 38(38;38;39) cm from starting ch. Place a marker at left-hand edge of work and **shape front**:
Next row: Keeping continuity of patt as set, work to last 3 sts, work 2 sts tog (1 dec), patt 1 st. Work a reverse row.
Next 4 rows: Patt as set to end.
Rep last 6 rows until 22(24;24;26) sts rem on hook. Work straight in patt as set until front matches back to shoulder, ending with a reverse row. Fasten off.

Right front
Work as given for left front from ** to **, setting patt for front panel as follows:
3rd row: Main patt 9(9;11;11) sts, 7 T-st, main patt 15(17;17;19) sts. Work to match left side, reversing front shaping.

Sleeves
Ch 34(34;36;36) and work in main patt as given for back. Inc 1 st at each end of 5th and every other 5th row until 58(60;64;64) sts on hook. Work straight until sleeve seam measures 49(49;51;51) cm from starting ch, ending with a reverse row. Fasten off.

To make up
Block pieces and pull into shape. Join shoulder seams. Set in sleeves. Sew sleeve and side seams.

Borders
With 5 mm crochet hook and RS facing, start at right side seam, keeping work flat, work 1 row of dc along lower edge of right front, up right front edge to shoulder (working 2 dc in 1 st at front marker), dc across back of neck, down left front edge and along lower edge of left front and back. Close rnd with 1 ss and work 3 dc in 1 st at front corners. Do not turn. Work 1 more rnd. Mark position of buttonholes with pins: the first 2 sts below marker at neck edge, the last 1,5 cm above lower edge, and rem 3 spaced between. Work a buttonhole by missing 2 sts and working 2 ch over missing sts. Shaping corners at lower edge of front and neck shaping, work 3 more rnds in dc. Close rnds with a ss. Fasten off. Work 4 rnds of dc around lower edge of sleeves as given for front and lower borders. Sew on buttons.

MEN'S BUTTON-NECK PULLOVER

Measurements
To fit: 91(97;102;107) cm chest
Garment measures: 97(102;107;112) cm
Length from shoulder: 64(66;68;70) cm
Sleeve seam: 54(54;55;55) cm

Materials
Maria Winter Tweed DK (50 g):
11(11;12;12) balls
One 8 mm TH
One pair of 3,25 mm knitting needles
3 buttons

Tension: 13 sts = 10 cm with TH over patt

Back
**With TH, ch 62(66;70;74) and work 1st and 2nd rows of T-st. Then cont in patt as follows:
3rd to 20th row: T-st.
21st to 30th row: T-kst. These 30 rows form patt. Rep patt from 3rd to 30th row until work measures 35(37;38;39) cm from starting ch, ending with a reverse row.

Shape armholes
Dec 6(6;7;7) sts at each end of next row. (At beg of row work 6(6;7;7) ss, at end of row leave 6(6;7;7) sts unworked.**) Cont over 50(54;56;60) sts until back measures 58(60;62;64) cm from starting ch, ending with a reverse row. Fasten off.

Front
Work as given for back from ** to **. Work 3(3;3;4) cm from armhole shaping, ending with a reverse row.

Divide for neck opening
Next row: Patt 22(24;25;27) sts, leaving rem sts unworked. Work straight in patt to complete left side of front until work measures 51(53;54;56) cm from starting ch, ending with a reverse row.

Shape neck
Next row: Patt to last 3 sts, leaving these sts unworked. Work a reverse row.
Next row: Patt to last 2(2;3;3) sts, leaving these sts unworked. Work a reverse row.
Dec 1 st at same edge in every forward row until 14(15;15;17) sts on hook. Cont in patt without shaping until front matches back to shoulder, ending with same reverse row of patt as back. Fasten off. With RS facing, return to rem sts, join yarn at neck division and work 6 ss over 6 centre sts, then cont in patt over 22(24;25;27) sts for right front until work measures 51(53;54;56) cm from starting ch. Shape neck as given for first side, working ss over the number of sts to be dec. Work to match left side. Fasten off.

Sleeves
Start from top. Ch 58(60;62;64) and work 1st and 2nd rows of T-st. Then work 10 rows in T-kst. Mark last row at both ends and cont in patt as given for back from 3rd to 30th row.
Next row: Dec 1 st at each end of row. Work a reverse row.
Next 6 rows: Patt to end.
Rep last 8 rows until 36(38;38;40) sts on hook. Cont in patt, without shaping, until sleeve seam measures 48(48;49;49) cm from starting ch. Fasten off.

Collar
With 3,25 mm knitting needles, cast on 121(121;129;129) sts and work in single rib [k1, p1] as follows:
1st row: On RS [k1, p1] to last st, k1.
2nd row: [P1, k1] to last st, p1.
Rep last 2 rows until work measures 8 cm, ending with 2nd row. Cast off in rib.

Button border
With RS facing and 3,25 mm knitting needles, pick up and k32 sts along front edge of front opening and work 11 rows in rib. Cast off in rib.

Buttonhole border
With RS facing and same knitting needles, pick up 32 sts along left front edge of neck opening and work 5 rows in rib.

Next row: Rib 2, *cast off 1 st, rib 11 (counting cast off sts). Rep from * once more, cast off 1 st, rib to end.
Next row: Rib to end, casting on 1 st over cast off st from previous row. Work 4 more rows and cast off in rib.

Cuffs
With knitting needles and RS facing, pick up and k43(47;47;49) sts along fastened off edge of sleeve and work 6 cm in rib as given for collar. Cast off in rib.

Front welt
With knitting needles and RS facing, pick up and k115(119;123;131) sts evenly along lower edge of front and work 6 cm in rib as given for collar. Cast off loosely in rib.

Back welt
Work as given for front.

To make up
Block pieces to measurements (except collar). Join shoulder and side seams. Join sleeves to markers. Set in sleeves. Overlap buttonhole border over button border and sew ends of borders to cast off sts at centre front. Sew on cast on edge of collar to neck edge, using an invisible st. Sew on buttons.

SOFT MOHAIR JACKET

Measurements

To fit: 91-97(102-107) cm bust
Garment measures: 106(116) cm
Length from shoulder: 62 cm (all sizes)
Sleeve seam: 47(48) cm

Materials

Patons Visions Mohair (50 g): 9(10) balls in M
2 balls in C1
1 ball in C2
One 8 mm TH
One 6 mm crochet hook
Shoulder pads (optional)

Tension: 12 sts = 10 cm with TH over T-st

Back

Starting sideways at right side seam.
Note: Carry only M loosely at side of work.
**Ch 71 in M and work 4 rows in T-st. Then cont in wave patt.
5th row: (C1) T-st.
6th row: (C1) T-st (reverse row).
7th row: (M) Ch 1 count as 1st tr, 1 T-tr (see instructions for Tunisian tr) in 2nd st from hook, *1 T-st into each of next 2 sts, slip 2 sts (= insert hook from right to left under vert thread of next 2 sts and without working these sts, slip them on hook), 1 T-st into each of next 2 sts, 1 T-tr into each of next 4 sts*. Rep from * to *, ending with only 3 T-tr.
8th row: (M) Reverse row.
9th and 10th row: (C1) T-st.
11th to 14th row: (M) T-st.
15th to 16th row: (C2) T-st.
17th row: (M) Miss 1st st (edge st), *2 T-st, 4 T-tr, 2 T-st, 2 ss*. Rep from * to * to end.
18th row: (M) Reverse row.
19th and 20th row: (C2) T-st.
21st to 24th row: (M) T-st.
25th to 30th row: As 5th to 10th row. Place a marker at right-hand edge of work**, and cont in M and T-st until work measures 17(20) cm from marker. Place a 2nd marker at same edge and cont in patt from 5th to 30th row. Work 4 more rows in M and T-st and fasten off.

Left front

Starting at side edge, work as given for back from ** to **. Join M into last st of reverse row and ch 10(12) for collar.
Next row: Collect 1 st from each ch and cont over 71 sts from front to end of row. Work a reverse row, 81(83) sts.
Cont in T-st to form collar until work measures 11(13) cm from marker, ending with a reverse row. Fasten off.

Right front

Starting at front edge with M, ch 81(83) and work 11(13) cm in T-st, ending with a reverse row.
Next row: Fasten off 10(12) sts (work 1 ss into each st) from collar, join C1 and work in wave patt over rem 71 sts from 5th to 30th row. Work 4 more rows in T-st and M. Fasten off.

Sleeves

Startting from top with M, ch 62 and work 2 rows in T-st. Change to C2 and work in wave patt from 15th to 30th row. Cont in M and T-st. At same time, keeping continuity of patt, dec 1 st at each end of 10th row and every following 4th row until 32(36) sts on hook. Work straight until sleeve measures 47(48) cm from starting ch, ending with a reverse row. Fasten off.

To make up

Block pieces to measurements. Join shoulder seams from side edge to markers. Using grafting st, join side edges of collar on WS. Sew collar to back of neck. Set in sleeves to match patt. Join side and sleeve seams.

Border

With 6 mm crochet hook and M, start at collar seam with RS facing, work 1 row of dc down from back of collar to lower edge, work 3 dc into 1 st at lower corner of front, cont in dc along lower edge of jacket, work 3 dc into 1 st at right front corner and work 1 row of dc up right side front to collar seam. Close rnd with a ss. Do not turn. Work 1 crab st into each dc of previous rnd, working 3 crab sts at each corner. Close rnd with a ss. Work 1 rnd each of dc and crab sts along lower edge of sleeves.

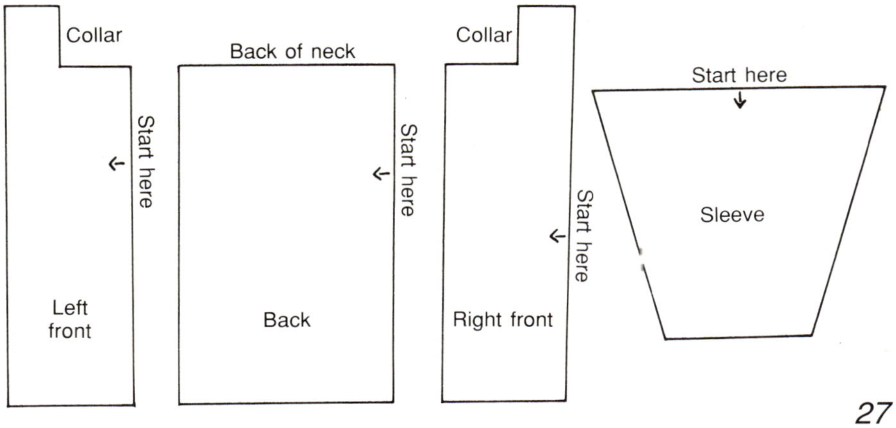

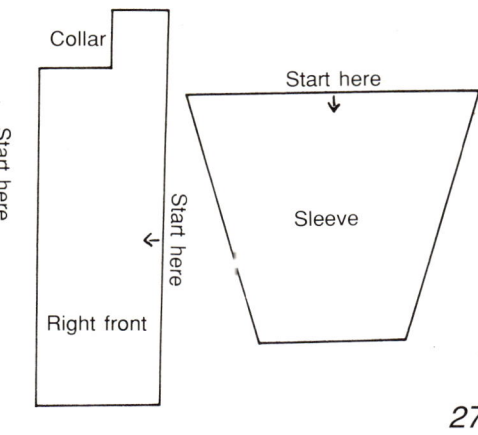

COUNTRY-STYLE CARDIGAN

Measurements
To fit: 81(86;91;96) cm bust
Garment measures: 86(91;96;102) cm
Length from shoulder: 53(54;56;57) cm
Sleeve seams: 46(46;47;48) cm

Materials
Pingouin Camargue (50 g): 7(8;9;9) balls
One 8 mm TH
One 4,5 mm crochet hook
5 buttons
Small amount of DK yarn in contrast shades for embroidery
Cord
One blunt embroidery needle

Tension: 13 sts = 10 cm with TH over T-st

Main part
Worked in 1 piece to armholes. With TH, ch 112(118;124;130) and work 25 cm in T-st, ending with a reverse row.

Divide for armholes
Right front: Work 25(27;28;30) sts in T-st, leaving rem sts unworked. Work a reverse row.
Next row: Work to last 3 sts, work 2 sts tog (1 dec), 1 T-st. Work a reverse row. Rep last 2 rows until 21(23;23;25) sts rem on hook. Cont straight until work measures 13(13;14;14) cm from armhole division, ending with a reverse row.

Shape neck
Dec 4 sts (work 1 ss into each of first 4 sts), T-st to end. Work a reverse row.
Next row: Dec 2 sts, T-st to end. Work a reverse row.
Rep last 2 rows, then dec 1 st at same edge until 11(12;12;14) sts on hook. Work straight until work measures 45(45;46;47) cm from starting ch, ending with a reverse row. Fasten off. With RS facing, rejoin yarn at armhole, work 1 ss into each of next 6 sts, work 50(52;56;58) T-st for back and leave rem sts unworked. Work a reverse row.

Back
Dec 2 sts at each end of next 2 forward rows. Dec 1 st at each end of every forward row until 42(44;46;48) sts on hook. Work straight to match right front to shoulder, ending with a reverse row. Fasten off. With RS facing, rejoin yarn to rem sts, work 1 ss into each of next 6 sts and cont over 25(27;28;30) sts.

Left front
Work a reverse row. Dec 2 sts at beg of next 2 forward rows, patt to end. Dec 1 st at same edge until 21(23;23;25) sts on hook and cont straight until left front matches right to neck.

Shape neck
Next row: Work in T-st to last 4 sts, leave sts unworked. Work a reverse row.
Next 2 forward rows: T-st to last 2 sts, leave sts unworked. Cont to dec 1 st at same edge until 11(12;12;14) sts on hook. Work straight to match right front to shoulder line. Fasten off.

Peplum
With RS facing, using TH and M, start at lower edge of left front, pick up 1 st from each lp ch until 112(118;124;130) sts on hook. Work a reverse row.
Next row: Miss 1st st on hook (edge st), work 1 T-st into each of next 3 sts, *1 T-pst into each of next 2 sts, 1 T-st into each of next 4 sts*. Rep from * to * to end. Work a reverse row. Rep last 2 rows twice more.
Next row: 4 T-st, inc 1 st, 1 T-pst into next st, inc 1 st, 1 T-pst into next st. Cont in 4 T-st, 4 T-pst to end of row, ending with 4 T-st. Cont in patt as set until peplum measures 8(9;10;10) cm, ending with a reverse row. Fasten off loosely.

Sleeves
Ch 28(32;32;34) and work 6 rows in T-st. Inc 1 st at each end of next forward row. Work a reverse row.
Next 4 rows: T-st.
Rep last 6 rows until 42(44;44;48) sts on hook. Work straight until sleeve measures 46(46;47;48) cm, ending with a reverse row.

Shape top
Next row: Dec 3 sts at each end of row (slip 3 sts at beg of row, leave 3 sts unworked at end of row). Work a reverse row. Dec 1 st at each end of every forward row until 16(18;18;18) sts rem on hook. Work straight until top of sleeve measures 15(16;16;17) cm from 1st dec, ending with a reverse row. Fasten off.

To make up
Block pieces to measurements. Using a length of yarn, work 1 ss into each unworked st from armhole and neck dec. Join shoulder seams. Join sleeve seams and set in sleeves, gathering extra fullness at shoulders.

Front and neck borders
With RS facing, using crochet hook and M, start at waistline, work 1 row of dc up right front to neck edge, work 3 dc into 1 st to form corner, work 1 row of dc around neck opening, work 3 sts into 1 st at left neck corner and cont in dc down left front edge to starting ch of main part (waistline). Turn. Ch 1 and work 1 dc into each dc of previous row. Turn. Mark position of buttonholes spaced evenly along right front between waistline and beg of neck shaping. For each buttonhole miss 2 dc, then cont in dc until all 5 buttonholes have been worked. Work to end of row, turn, ch 1 and work a row of dc, working 2 ch over each buttonhole. Using contrast colour, work 1 row of crab st. Work 1 rnd dc and 1 rnd crab st in contrast colour at lower edge of sleeves. Sew on buttons. Crochet or twist one cord in contrast colour about 150 cm long and pass between sts at waistline. Embroider front flowers, following illustration and work in lazy daisy st and bullion knot st with thread wound around needle 8 times for centre bullions and 14 times for other bullions. Use French knot for centre of lazy daisy flower.

ELEGANT EDGE-TO-EDGE JACKET

Measurements
To fit: 86(91;97;102) cm bust
Length from shoulder: 50(51;52;52) cm
Sleeve seam: 45(45;46;46) cm

Materials
Pingouin Mosaic Brushed Chunky (50 g): 7(7;8;8) balls in M
Pingouin Stardust (silver) (50 g): 4(4;4;5) balls in C
One 8 mm TH
One 4,5 mm crochet hook
2 shoulder pads

Note: *Pingouin Stardust* can be substituted with any DK yarn.

Tension: 15 sts = 10 cm with TH over patt

Back
With M and TH, ch 68(70;78;82) and work in patt as follows:
1st row: (M) As 1st row of T-st. Join C into last st.
2nd row: (C) As 2nd row of T-st.
3rd row: (C) As 3rd row of T-st.
4th row: (M) As 2nd row of T-st.
5th row: (M) As 3rd row of T-st.
2nd to 5th row form patt st and are rep throughout.
Note: Carry yarn not in use loosely at left-hand edge of work.
Work in patt until back measures 30 cm from starting ch, ending with a reverse row in M.

Shape armholes
**Dec 4 sts at each end of row (work 4 ss at beg of row and leave 4 sts unworked at end of row). Work a reverse row.
Dec 1 st at each end of every forward row until 52(54;60;64) sts on hook. Work straight in patt until back measures 50(51;52;52) cm from starting ch, ending with a reverse row in M. Fasten off.

Right front
With M, ch 34(36;40;42) and work in patt as given for back until work measures 30 cm from starting ch, ending with same reverse row as given for back.

Shape armhole
Next row: Patt to last 4 sts, leaving these sts unworked. Work a reverse row.
Dec 1 st at same edge until 26(28;31;33) sts rem on hook. Work straight until front measures about 8 cm less than back to shoulder, ending with a reverse row in M.

Shape neck
Next row: Work 1 ss into each of 1st 4 sts, patt to end. Work a reverse row.
Next 3 forward rows: Work 1 ss into each of 1st 2 sts. Dec 1 st at neck edge until 17(18;20;21) sts rem on hook. Work straight until front matches back to shoulder, ending with same patt row.

Left front
Work as given for right front, reversing shapings.

Sleeves
With M, ch 38(38;40;40) and work in patt as given for back for 4 cm.
Next row: Ch 1 counting as a st, work 1st st from edge (1 inc), patt to last st, work 1 st into top of ch between last 2 sts (1 inc), patt last st. This is an invisible way of inc when working in striped patt. Work a reverse row.
Next 4 rows: Patt to end.
Rep last 6 rows until 54(58;58;60) sts on hook, ending with a reverse row in M.

Shape sleeve top
Dec 4 sts at each end of next row as given for back from **. Dec 1 st at each end of every forward row until 18(20;20;20) sts rem on hook. Work straight until sleeve top measures 17(18;18;19) cm from first dec, ending with a reverse row in M. Fasten off.

To make up
Using matching thread, work ss over all sts left unworked from armhole and neck shapings. Block pieces to measurements. Join shoulder seams. Set in sleeves, matching up stripes to gathered top, taking any fullness to sleeve top. Join side and sleeve seams.

Lower border
With RS facing, using M and 4,5 mm crochet hook, start at lower edge of right front, work 1 dc into each vert thread along lower edge of fronts and back. *Turn, ch 1, work 1 dc into each dc of previous row, rep from * twice more. Fasten off.

Front and neck borders
With RS facing, using M and 4,5 mm crochet hook, start at lower edge of right front, work about 58(60;62;62) dc up right front edge to neck edge, work 3 dc into 1 st at corner and work 50 dc around neck edge, work 3 dc into 1 dc at neck corner and work about 58(60;62;62) dc down left front edge, turn, ch 1 and work 3 more rows in dc as given for lower border. Fasten off. With RS facing, using C and 4,5 mm crochet hook, start at side edge, work 1 row dc into each dc of previous row, close rnd with a ss. Do not turn. Ch 1 and work 1 row in crab st. Fasten off.

Sleeve edge
Starting at sleeve seam with RS facing, work as given for front borders, 3 rnds in M, 1 rnd in C and 1 rnd in crab st. Fasten off. Sew in shoulder pads.